DILBERT DILBERT DILBERT DILBERT
DILBERT DILBERT DILBERT DILBERT D
DILBERT DILBERT DILBERT DILBERT
DILBERT DILBERT

DILBERT DILBERT DILBERT
DILBERT DILBERT DILBERT D
DILBERT DILBERT
DILBERT DILBERT
DILBERT DILBERT
DILBERT DILBERT
DILBERT DILBERT DILBERT
DILBERT DILBERT DILBERT
DILBERT DILBERT DILBERT DILBERT
DILBERT DILBERT DILBERT DILBERT
DILBERT DILBERT DILBERT DILBERT
DILBERT DILBERT DILBERT DILBERT DIL
DILBERT DILBERT DILBERT DILBERT
L B E R T DILBERT DILBERT
DILBERT DILBERT DILBERT DILBERT
DILBERT DILBERT
DILBERT DILBERT

COMMUNICATION IS GOOD!

FOR _____

FROM _____

TELLING IT LIKE IT ISN'T.

A DILBERT™ BOOK
BY
SCOTT ADAMS

ANDREWS AND MCMEEL
A UNIVERSAL PRESS SYNDICATE COMPANY
KANSAS CITY

ISBN: 0-8362-1324-6

YOU DON'T ADD MUCH TO A CONVERSATION, BUT YOU'RE EASILY THE BEST LISTENER I'VE EVER MET.
AAAEE!

I'M SO LUCKY TO BE DATING YOU, LIZ. YOU'RE AT LEAST AN EIGHT.
YOU'RE A TEN.

ARE WE USING THE SAME SCALE?
TEN IS THE NUMBER OF SECONDS IT WOULD TAKE TO REPLACE YOU.

WOULD WE GET BONUSES FOR WORKING HARDER?
THIS MUST BE THE SLOW CLASS.

I'M GOING TO START MY OWN BOOK PUBLISHING COMPANY SO I CAN REJECT PEOPLE ALL DAY LONG.

I'LL DISMISS THEIR LIFE'S WORK WITH A GESTURE AND A WITTY COMMENT.

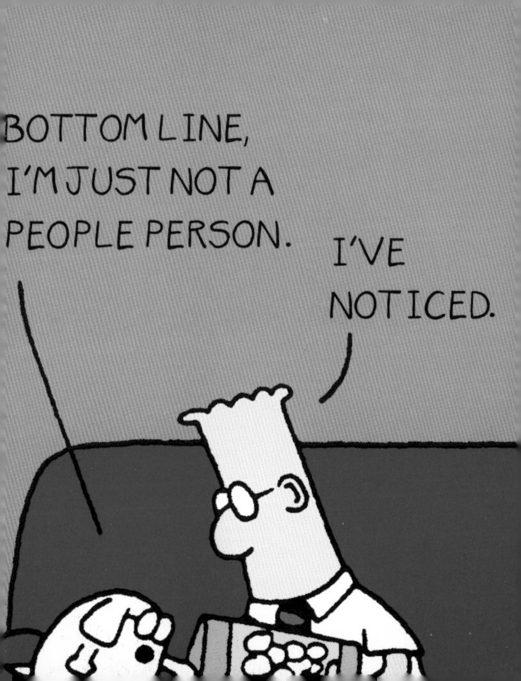
BOTTOM LINE, I'M JUST NOT A PEOPLE PERSON.
I'VE NOTICED.

I DIDN'T KNOW YOU
WERE THE DIRECTOR OF
PRODUCT ENHANCEMENTS.

IN THIS SENSITIVITY EXERCISE, CLOSE YOUR EYES AND IMAGINE HOW IT FEELS TO BE A WOMAN.
PEOPLE ACKNOWLEDGE MY EXISTENCE. THEY SMILE FOR NO REASON AND HOLD THE DOOR OPEN. I'M...I'M POPULAR.
I CAN'T FIND MY KEYS.

I'M NEVER GOING BACK. I CAN'T. I WON'T.
MY BLOUSE FALLS TO THE FLOOR...
BREAK! BREAK!

LET'S GO AROUND THE TABLE AND GIVE AN UPDATE ON EACH OF OUR PROJECTS.

MY PROJECT IS A PATHETIC SERIES OF POORLY PLANNED, NEAR-RANDOM ACTS. MY LIFE IS A TRAGEDY OF EMOTIONAL DESPERATION.

IT'S MORE OR LESS CUSTOMARY TO SAY THINGS ARE GOING FINE.
I THINK I NEED A HUG.

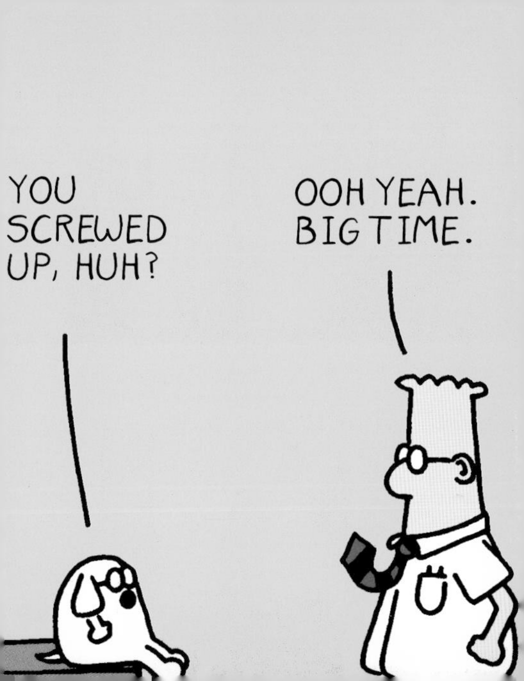
YOU SCREWED UP, HUH?
OOH YEAH. BIG TIME.

I THINK YOU CAN RELATE TO THIS SCENE.
AM I THE SEAGULL OR THE CLAM?

IS THERE SOMEBODY LESS EXPERIENCED I COULD TALK TO?
DO YOU HAVE MY BOSS'S NUMBER?

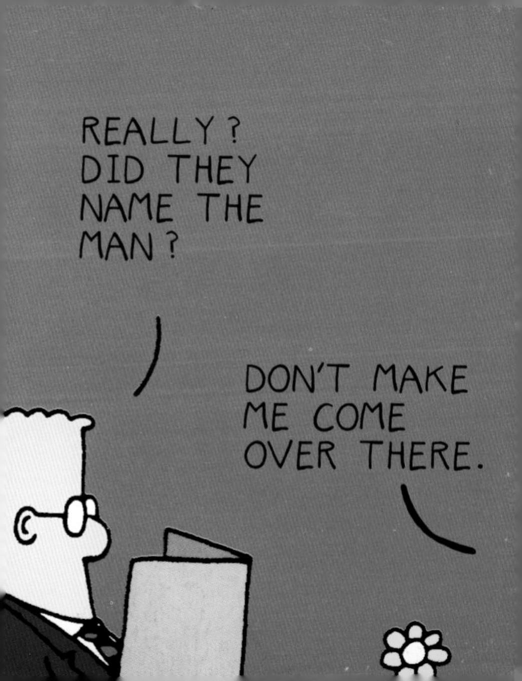
REALLY? DID THEY NAME THE MAN?
DON'T MAKE ME COME OVER THERE.

WON'T PEOPLE SHOW YOUR VIEWPOINT TO BE FLAWED BY VIRTUE OF THEIR INTELLIGENT QUESTIONS?
LIKE THAT ONE?

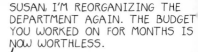

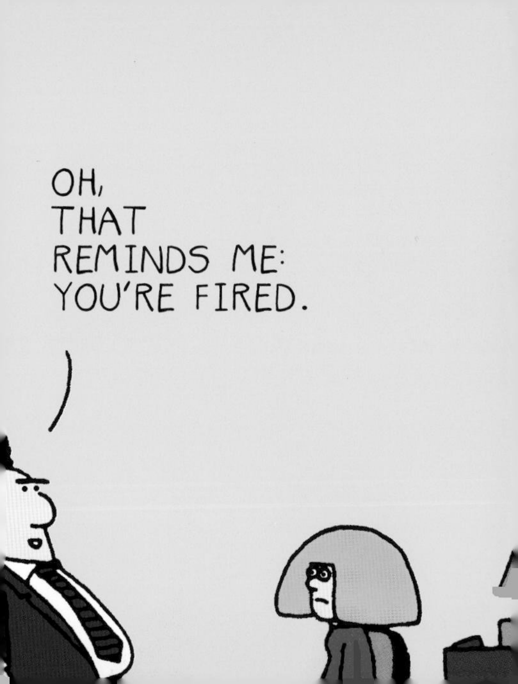
OH, THAT REMINDS ME: YOU'RE FIRED.

WE'RE DUMBER THAN SQUIRRELS. WE HEAR VOICES AND DO WHAT THEY COMMAND. I HAVE BROCCOLI IN MY SOCKS.
GOOD WRITING.
THANKS

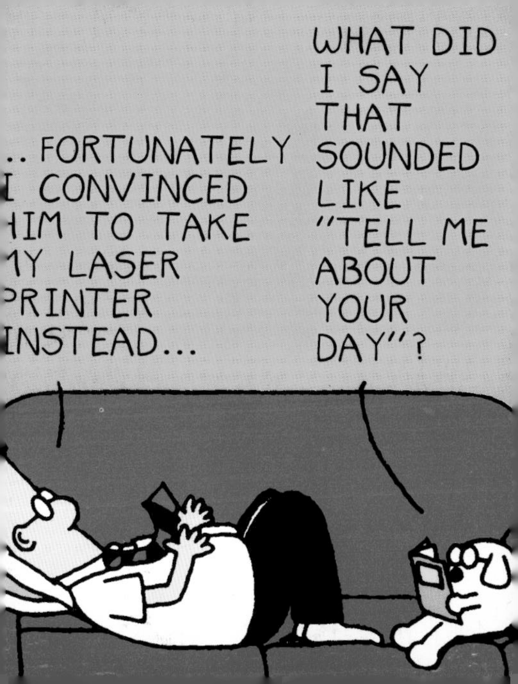
.. FORTUNATELY I CONVINCED HIM TO TAKE MY LASER PRINTER INSTEAD...
WHAT DID I SAY THAT SOUNDED LIKE "TELL ME ABOUT YOUR DAY"?

I STILL DON'T
UNDERSTAND WOMEN,
BUT I THINK WHEN
THEY YELL "HAAIII"
IT MEANS THEY
LIKE THE DRESS
THEY'RE WEARING.

RATBERT, DID YOU KNOW THAT YOUR BRAIN AUTOMATICALLY COORDINATES MILLIONS OF ACTIVITIES EVERY SECOND?

IMAGINE IF IT GOT JUST A LITTLE BIT CONFUSED—ALL THOSE NEURONS FIRING RANDOMLY...

TELLING IT LIKE
IT ISN'T